At the Top of Their Game

Neymar

Superstar Striker

Ruth Bjorklund

Cavendish Square
New York

Published in 2020 by Cavendish Square Publishing, LLC
243 5th Avenue, Suite 136, New York, NY 10016

First Edition

Library of Congress Cataloging-in-Publication Data

Names: Bjorklund, Ruth author.
Title: Neymar : superstar striker / Ruth Bjorklund.
Description: First Edition. | New York : Cavendish Square, 2020. | Series: At the top of their game | Audience: Grade level for this book is grades 9-12. | Includes bibliographical references and index. |
Identifiers: LCCN 2019014245 (print) | LCCN 2019019539 (ebook) |
ISBN 9781502651037 (ebook) | ISBN 9781502651020 (library bound) |
ISBN 9781502651006 (pbk.) | ISBN 9781502651013 (6 pack)
Subjects: LCSH: Neymar, 1992- —Juvenile literature. |
Soccer players—Brazil—Biography—Juvenile literature.
Classification: LCC GV942.7.N455 (ebook) | LCC GV942.7.N455
B76 2020 (print) | DDC 796.334092 [B] --dc23
LC record available at https://lccn.loc.gov/2019014245

Editor: Jodyanne Benson
Copy Editor: Michele Suchomel-Casey
Associate Art Director: Alan Sliwinski
Designer: Joe Parenteau
Production Coordinator: Karol Szymczuk
Photo Research: J8 Media

The photographs in this book are used by permission and through the courtesy of: Cover Robbie Jay Barratt-AMA/Getty Images; pp. 4, 6-7, 62-63 AGIF/Shutterstock.com; p. 10 Foto Arena LTDA/ Alamy Stock Photo; pp. 13, 90-91 Fabrice Coffrini/AFP/Getty Images; pp. 16-17 Benilson Tavares/ Shutterstock.com; pp. 20-21 Muhammad Hanif MM/Shutterstock.com; p. 23 John Spence/Sipa/AP Images; p. 28 Miguel Schincariol/AFP/Getty Images; p. 30 Popperfoto/Getty Images; pp. 34-35 Will Rodrigues/Shutterstock.com; p. 38 Red Bull/AP Images; p. 40 Christian Liewig/Corbis Sport/Getty Images; pp. 42, 45 Tim Clayton/Corbis Sport/Getty Images; pp. 48-49 Helio Suenaga/LatinContent WO/Getty Images; p. 51 Stuart Franklin/FIFA/Getty Images; p. 57 ©AP Images; p. 59 Aflo Co. Ltd./Alamy Stock Photo; p. 64 Ira L. Black/Corbis Sport/Getty Images; p. 69 Mike Hewitt/FIFA/Getty Images; pp. 70-71, 86 Aurelien Meunier/Getty Images; pp. 77, 82 Jean Catuffe/ Getty Images; p. 80 Dave Winter/Icon Sport/Getty Images; p. 88 Anadolu Agency/Getty Images.

Printed in the United States of America

At the Top of Their Game

Contents

CBF
10

Introduction

Who Is Neymar?

In 1992, a star was born to a small family living in Mogi das Cruzes, which is on the outskirts of São Paulo, Brazil. It was a humble beginning for a man whose name would someday be known throughout the world. A soccer player extraordinaire, Neymar da Silva Santos Jr. has become one of the world's greatest athletes.

As a testament to his talent and fame, Neymar is known worldwide by just his first name. To family and friends, he is also called Juninho, which means "junior" in Portuguese. Portuguese is the official language of Brazil.

A Passion for Soccer

Like many kids around the world, Neymar was obsessed with soccer. It is a game you can play with just a ball and a couple of sticks to make a goal. You do not need a special field or expensive equipment. Many kids without the money to buy balls will make them from paper, rags, plastic bags, string, rubber tires, or anything else that can

Opposite: As captain of the Brazilian national team, Neymar celebrated a victory over South American rival Chile.

Neymar takes a penalty shot during a World Cup match against Croatia.

be made into a round shape and kicked. Neymar, although he was fortunate enough to have his own soccer balls, played soccer with his friends in the pebbly, dusty streets of his neighborhood.

His parents were devoted to him and encouraged his love of the sport. His father had briefly played professional soccer for a local team. His father, Neymar Sr., is known as Neymar Pai. *Pai* means "father" in Portuguese.

Neymar Pai spotted his son's talent at a very young age. He knew that in Brazil and elsewhere many kids dreamed of playing soccer professionally. Those dreams, however, rarely became a reality. However, from early on, Neymar Pai thought his boy might have what it takes to succeed.

Getting Noticed

Neymar did catch the eye of other adults in the soccer world. In fact, they told Neymar's father that they wanted to coach him and see how far the boy could go. Neither Neymar Pai nor Neymar's mother, Nadine, wanted to stand in his way. However, they thought the boy was too young. Besides, they did not have enough money for Neymar to play.

However, Neymar got started on his future soon enough. He played on indoor teams designed for children. He moved up to junior leagues. By the time he was a young teen, he was actively recruited for FIFA under-16 and under-17 teams. FIFA stands for Fédération Internationale de Football Association (the French phrase meaning International Federation of Association Football). In most countries, soccer is called football.

Soccer became Neymar's life. He was a good teammate with a range of skills. After playing many positions on the soccer field, or pitch, Neymar's coaches decided his best fit was as a striker.

A striker is the player who usually scores the most goals in a game. As such, strikers are often teams' stars. (Although, sometimes, strikers who miss their goal shots get booed.)

Opponents became increasingly wary of Neymar's playing ability. Defenders on the opponents' teams did their best to keep Neymar from coming out from the sidelines and taking the ball away from them.

Neymar is athletic and a quick thinker on the pitch. His exceptional talent carried him into professional leagues. He has played for his hometown, for his state, and on national and international teams.

Not only does Neymar thrill his fans with his extraordinary skill, but he also stays in the spotlight with dramatic antics on the field and attention-getting behavior off the field. Many sports commentators say Neymar's theatrics may be overblown, and in some cases, his actions off the pitch have created scandals and controversies. Despite these things, millions of soccer fans believe that Neymar's exciting style and skill have earned him a rightful place on the world's stage.

Chapter 1

A Child Star

Neymar, the future world-famous soccer star, began life under the cloud of a family trauma. The trauma led to financial struggles for his family, but his family was loving and supportive of each other. Although they had little money, they did not lack for ambition, hope, and determination. Neymar's parents saw early that their son was someone special, and they did everything they could to help him find his way.

Life in Mogi das Cruzes

Neymar Pai, Neymar's father, loved soccer. He began his career playing on a juniors team belonging to Santos, one of São Paulo's professional teams. When he was sixteen, he was talented enough to play professionally for a club called Portuguesa Santista. Later, he played for a number of other clubs before joining his hometown team in Mogi das Cruzes. The team paid for a comfortable apartment for Neymar Pai and his wife, Nadine Goncalves.

Opposite: Today, Neymar is known wherever he goes. He is shown here hosting a gala. However, he came from humble beginnings.

Mogi das Cruzes is a noisy, bustling city. Traffic is chaotic, with commuters going into São Paulo to work. Buses spew diesel fumes, trains are crowded, drivers honk at each other continuously, and motorcycles and bicycles zip in and out. Many roads are steep, and in poorer neighborhoods, the roads are unpaved. Dust flies everywhere. Many people live on very little money. However, there are jobs in agriculture—vegetable farms and orchid fields—and in services such as health care and retail businesses. Large factories make car parts, tractors, and steel construction equipment. There are tall apartment buildings, small tin-roofed houses, and modest suburban homes with small yards. There are few parks or soccer fields; many children play in the street.

A New Family

Neymar Pai and Nadine were eager to start a family. They welcomed a baby boy on February 5, 1992, and they named him Neymar da Silva Santos Jr. Neymar Pai and Nadine looked forward to providing a good home for themselves and their child. As a professional soccer player, Neymar Pai was paid well. In Mogi das Cruzes, he played the best soccer of his career. He bought his parents a house in São Vicente, a pleasant suburb of the city of São Paulo, as well as a nice car for himself.

The house that Neymar Pai purchased for his parents and the car that he purchased for himself would become significant in ways no one would have imagined. In June 1992, just four months after Neymar was born, the family went to visit Neymar's grandparents. Night was closing in, and rain was falling. The drive between Mogi das Cruzes and São Vicente was along a dangerous mountain road. As Neymar Pai rounded a sharp curve, a car coming from the

Neymar stands between his parents, Nadine and Neymar Pai.

opposite direction swerved into their lane. The crash was sudden and unavoidable. The family's car careened off the road and came to a halt dangling from the edge of a steep cliff. Neymar Pai's legs were crushed under the steering wheel. He could not move. He and Nadine were in a panic about their baby boy in the back seat. Through sheer force of will, Nadine smashed the back window and crawled out. She frantically searched for Neymar. When help arrived, rescuers found him surprisingly unharmed, with just a scratch on his forehead.

The near fatal crash changed everything for Neymar's family. His father spent a year in a hospital and rehabilitation center. He feared he would never walk again, and he was certain he would never play soccer again. However, Neymar Pai was determined to care for his family. He regained most of his strength and joined a new professional soccer club, but he would never be the player he once was.

Neymar's sister, Rafaella, was born in 1996. Now a family of four, Neymar Pai and Nadine struggled to pay the bills. Very often, they went without electricity and used candles at night.

When Neymar was very young, Neymar Pai decided to leave Mogi das Cruzes and move his family in with his parents in São Vicente. However, the house was not built to accommodate another family. Although the family was stuck in cramped quarters and didn't have a lot of money, they remained happy and loving. In São Vicente, Neymar Pai worked three jobs—as a salesperson, a truck driver, and a car mechanic. Nadine worked as a cook in a child care center.

The Early Years

Neymar was barely walking before he started playing with a soccer ball. Neymar Pai played with him in the house and was amused to see that his little boy could catch and pass the ball not only with his hands, but also with his feet. Neymar collected soccer balls like other toddlers collected teddy bears. He slept with one in his bed at night. At one point, Nadine counted fifty-four soccer balls in Neymar's cramped room. She also recounts the time when Neymar was two years old, and they were shopping at an outdoor market. Neymar spotted a little yellow ball and tore away from his mother. He chased the ball across the street, and he was nearly mowed down by cars.

In his grandparents' tiny house, Neymar found ways to set up soccer drills. He moved furniture in order to create obstacles to dribble around. He made his cousins and his sister (when she was old enough) play against him—as defenders and goalkeepers. Eventually, he was old enough to play outdoors in the street with the neighborhood children. The older children took a look at skinny little Neymar and refused to let him play. However, like his determined father, Neymar convinced the older boys he was their equal. At age five, he was scoring goals and playing street soccer with boys twice his age.

Neymar was a good student. He was always cheerful and friendly but a little bit shy. However, he was not the least bit shy when it came to playing soccer. As soon as the school bell rang, Neymar and his friends raced out to play soccer. They played on the street, which was on a hillside. Teams had to switch sides every few matches to make the playing field fair. One year, Neymar Pai splurged and planted

After financial setbacks, Neymar's family moved in with his grandparents in São Vicente, in the Brazilian state of São Paulo.

grass on their small lawn. He wanted to give Neymar a real pitch to play on. Once the new grass sprouted, Neymar invited neighborhood children over to play. They played soccer until dark. By the end of the day, the new lawn had turned to mud. Neymar knew his father would be angry, so for two weeks he pretended to be asleep before his father came home from work. Finally, his guilt got the better of him, and Neymar faced his father, got a deserved scolding, and apologized. He also apologized to his mother quite regularly, for Neymar was constantly playing soccer in the house. He used the doorway to his room or the legs of a chair to make goals. He thrashed up against furniture to foul an imaginary opponent. He kicked the ball, he chested the ball, and he headed the ball. He frequently broke lamps, vases, and pottery. Nadine forgave her son many times. She had long understood her son was particularly driven. After all, it was she who gave Neymar his first soccer ball, at age two.

The Next Step

Neymar, Rafaella, and their mother were regular fans at Neymar Pai's soccer matches. Although Neymar was crazy about soccer, it was hard for him to sit still and just watch. He usually entertained himself by running up and the down the bleachers. He was so fleet-footed and graceful that it seemed he was simply running on a flat track. One day, while Neymar was scrambling about, he was spotted by Betinho dos Santos, a soccer scout and coach. The coach was impressed by how agile Neymar was. He was quick and athletic. He noted that both of Neymar's parents were also very fit. Betinho thought Neymar had a lot of potential.

Betinho was putting together a youth soccer club in São Vicente, and he wanted Neymar to join. He waited until after Neymar Pai's match ended and asked if Neymar could go with him and try out for the youth team. Neymar Pai and Nadine agreed. Neymar was only six.

Betinho brought Neymar to a team trial. Betinho remarked later that the first time he saw Neymar touch a soccer ball his heart started pounding. He felt like he was looking at a soccer genius. Even though he was so young, Betinho said that Neymar already had an individual style. He was imaginative and clever. He could kick with an accuracy extremely rare for someone his age. Neymar could dribble with speed and was fearless about taking on opposing defenders.

Betinho began developing the boy's skills right away. Neymar was a small, skinny, wiry kid. He needed to build strength and stamina. Betinho spent hours with Neymar, coaching him in a variety of strength-building exercises. Betinho was also careful to keep the training drills from souring Neymar's love of the game. He decided to put Neymar on a futsal team. Futsal is a sport that is like a smaller version of soccer. Nearly all of Brazil's star professional soccer players started out on a futsal team.

Futsal

Futsal is an indoor soccer-like game, played on a hard court about the size of a basketball court. The game is shorter—two twenty-minute halves and a five-minute halftime. (A soccer game has two forty-five-minute halves and a fifteen-minute halftime.) The ball is smaller and heavier, with less bounce. There are four players and one goalkeeper on each side. (A soccer game has ten players and one goalkeeper on each side.) Fewer players means that there are more opportunities to touch the ball. Players also play both offense

These young people are playing futsal, a type of soccer played on a hard surface with just five members on each team.

and defense. In the smaller space, players have to think quickly and creatively. They learn how to be more accurate in their passing and shooting. They learn how to dribble with both feet and zoom in and out around their opponents.

There are some different rules in futsal versus soccer. One difference is contact with opposing players is much more limited. For example, no shoulder charges are allowed in futsal. Futsal originated in Brazil in 1933, but now it is played around the world. Today, FIFA sponsors international futsal competitions.

Coach Betinho took Neymar under his wing. He began letting Neymar compete in futsal matches. When he took Neymar to play in his first futsal tournament, their team won. Neymar was the leading goal-scorer of the entire event. Betinho also took Neymar along with him to the other teams that he coached, including Portuguesa Santista, one of Neymar Pai's former clubs. Watching the other teams, Neymar paid serious attention. He learned to recognize where and how the ball would move, given any player's kick or pass. At his own team practices, Neymar was the first player to arrive and the last to leave. Neymar then joined Portuguesa Santista's youth team.

Coach Betinho and others who had seen Neymar play confided in Neymar Pai and Nadine that their son could become one of Brazil's greatest soccer players. Although the da Silva Santos family lived on a tight budget, they were willing to support their son in every way that they could. They attended his matches, both home and away. They provided money for uniforms and good soccer boots. They instilled discipline and made sure that he did his homework. They were determined that he would be a successful student and still have ample time to practice.

Neymar Pai stands proudly as his son is introduced onto the pitch.

When Neymar was not officially practicing with his team, he played soccer at home with his father. Although Neymar Pai was not as talented as his son would be, he was a good player and a patient teacher. Neymar Pai had great dribbling and ball-handling skills. As a professional, he played both forward and striker. At one point, Neymar Pai was so valued by his fans that they established a private fund to provide him with housing and a better salary than his club could offer.

Neymar Pai's body never fully recovered from the accident. In 1997, he played his last professional game, but he remained a very important figure in the world of professional soccer when he became his son's manager. Neymar has said of his father, "He is sometimes harsh with me, but everything he does, he does for me, for us. For our family." Many of Neymar's coaches have said that Neymar Pai was instrumental in helping Neymar achieve success. They have commented on Neymar Pai's insistence that Neymar learn to respect his coaches and teammates and to work hard.

Portuguesa Santista

After playing futsal, Neymar was invited by Coach Betinho to join a traveling team: Portuguesa Santista. The coach took Neymar and a few of his other good players to play friendly games. When he thought they were ready, Betinho entered the team into a tournament. Neymar was only eleven; his teammates and opponents were at least twelve. It was the first official time Neymar competed with eleven on a side and on a full-size pitch.

Neymar played on the left side. He darted in front of the defense and captured the ball. He dribbled rings around them before passing to another teammate or going for the goal himself. In the final game,

Neymar got the ball in a seemingly impossible situation, passed it, had it passed back to him, and shot for the upper net of the goal. Coach Betinho called it a "masterpiece."

The most memorable game of the tournament was between Portuguesa Santista and São Paulo. Portuguesa Santista was not expected to win, but they did: 4–1. Neymar scored two of the goals. It was their third win, which put Portuguesa Santista on top of the league. São Paulo coaches were so impressed that they begged Neymar to join their team, but Neymar stayed with his team.

School

Reginaldo Ferreira de Oliveira, known as Fino, was a coach at Portuguesa Santista and a futsal coordinator at a private school. Fino was wowed by Neymar's play. He was especially impressed by Neymar's ability to quickly jump from futsal to regulation play. Fino knew that Neymar's family did not have a lot of money, but he wanted to give Neymar more opportunities to succeed. The private school he worked at, Liceu São Paulo, was very expensive, so Fino talked to the school administrators. He explained that Neymar would easily be a star on the school's futsal team.

The school agreed to let Neymar try out for the team. Neymar's tryout convinced the administrators that, without a doubt, Neymar would be a great asset to the school. They knew a good futsal team would attract more students and improve the school's reputation. Neymar (along with his sister Rafaella) was granted a full scholarship. The scholarship included school fees, uniforms, books, and transportation.

At Liceu São Paulo, Neymar was an average student. His best subjects were history and physical education. Math was a challenge, but given the work ethic instilled in Neymar by his parents, he studied hard. He had excellent attendance. He was respectful and polite to teachers and other students.

Soccer remained his passion. Even when soccer was not allowed during the school day, Neymar managed to find a way around it. He and his friends would skip lunch to play soccer. During study periods, Neymar sometimes went to the headmaster and begged to be given a ball to practice shots. When they thought they could get away with it, Neymar and his friends snuck off to the gym and pulled down the volleyball nets to play futsal.

The school's administrators knew they had made the right choice to take a chance on Neymar. Other schools were envious. Some of them tried to lure Neymar away. One school accused Liceu São Paulo of accepting Neymar only to play soccer and of not enrolling him in academic classes. Of course, that was not true, but the school headmaster had to bring paperwork to prove otherwise.

A Young Star

Neymar had already earned a reputation for excellence on the pitch. Soccer fans, especially other students around the city, knew who he was. Liceu futsal matches were well attended. Even the local newspapers started to write about the rising star that was Neymar.

In 2003, the powerful club Santos FC (the FC stands for Football Club, or Futebol Clube in Portuguese) convinced Neymar to join their youth academy. After school and futsal practice, Neymar headed over to the Santos training grounds and practiced until dark.

Neymar was his school's star player. However, he had become extremely busy, keeping up with schoolwork, futsal practice, and practice with the Santos club. Neymar frequently made the choice to focus on Santos and not school. He regularly skipped after-school futsal practice. His fellow student teammates were jealous that he was not penalized by the coach.

One day, the coach insisted that Neymar attend after-school practice. Neymar came, darted and dribbled around everyone, scored from midfield, and made dozens of goals and free kicks. He was so superior that his teammates and his coach had to acknowledge Neymar could miss practice and still excel. They also admitted that their team, with Neymar playing, was one of the best around.

Each year, a media organization called Tribuna awards a trophy, the Copa Tribuna de Futsal Escolar, to the best school team. At least eighty schools from around the state of São Paulo participate in the tournament. The games are broadcast on Tribuna television. The first year Neymar and his closest friend Dudu played on the team, they lost in the final. However, it had been a very long time since the school had advanced that far.

In 2003, they won the cup. When Neymar was shown on television holding the Tribuna Cup over his head, his fame grew like wildfire. Newspapers and sportscasters started to follow him. One headline declared, "Neymar could be the next national hero." This moment would mark the beginning of his soccer success.

Chapter 2

The Youth Academy

The year 2003 was a pivotal year for Neymar. His team had won a major school trophy. He was recruited by the Santos soccer club to enter their youth academy. He also changed schools. Neymar was only eleven years old, and his future was already looking very bright.

Santos FC

Santos FC had tried to recruit Neymar in 2002. However, Neymar Pai intervened, saying that Neymar was young and still needed the support of Coach Betinho and Portuguesa Santista. In 2003, Santos finally convinced Neymar Pai to allow Neymar to join the Santos youth academy. Neymar Pai agreed on the condition that Betinho would be hired at Santos as a youth team coach.

Santos FC was established by athletes in 1912. Many teams already existed in the state, but the Santos players wanted a team that represented the spirit of their working-class neighborhood. They played and won their first match and were invited to the Liga

Opposite: As a young teenager, Neymar already showed signs of greatness.

Paulista Futebol, which is the name of São Paulo's soccer league. They lost in that first professional tournament, and thereafter, whenever Santos played city rivals, the players were greeted with shouts of "Rotten fish! Fishmongers!" Finally, at one match, the team was so tired of the name-calling that their captain shouted back, "We are fishmongers, and we are proud of it!" From that day on, the Santos team has been affectionately nicknamed "Peixe,"

Shown here in 1961, Santos FC's forward Pelé is one of the most famous soccer players of all time.

which is Portuguese for "fish." The Peixe chose the orca, or killer whale, as their mascot.

Today, Santos is one of the most successful soccer clubs in Brazil. Santos's star first shone brightly in the 1960s when a host of brilliant players joined the team. The most magnificent player was Edson Arantes do Nascimento (known as Pelé), who was named Athlete of the Twentieth Century by the International Olympic Committee. Pelé played his entire career, beginning at age sixteen, in the Santos organization and brought worldwide recognition to the "fishmongers" of Santos. Santos began winning trophy after trophy, nationally and internationally. It was the first team ever to achieve ten thousand goals scored.

By the late 1990s, however, Santos was in decline. Many of their best players had left. The team owners decided to rebuild Santos and focus on their youth academy and junior team. It was with that in mind that a team official named Jose Ely de Miranda, known as Zito, became interested in an eleven-year-old futsal player named Neymar. Zito attended a Portuguesa Santista match and saw that Neymar could play a huge role in rebuilding Santos. After much bargaining, Neymar signed a contract and enrolled in the Santos FC Academy in 2003. Zito remarked that watching Neymar play filled him with joy.

After Neymar Pai gave Neymar the go-ahead to sign with Santos FC, he decided the family should move to Santos to support his son's growing career. Santos, the city, was a far cry from Neymar's birthplace, Mogi das Cruzes. It is a bustling city with a major seaport, the largest in all of Latin America. It was once the coffee-trading capital of the world. Portuguese architecture and art tell the story of the people who called this city home. In the style of their homeland, the Portuguese-constructed buildings are

Neymar Pai: Father, Coach, and Best Friend

To pursue his goals, Neymar could not have had more support than what he received from his father, Neymar da Silva Santos, known as Neymar Pai. As a former professional soccer player himself, he knew how to coax the best from his son. Whenever it was in the best interests of Neymar's career, Neymar Pai worked overtime. Neymar Pai sacrificed for his son and the rest of his family. When Neymar moved between teams, Neymar Pai moved the family. Neymar Pai took over the role of agent in 2012. At every contract signing, Neymar Pai was present to be sure that Neymar received the best deal.

Neymar Pai instilled in his son an incredible work ethic as well as the qualities of honesty, respect, and kindness. He encouraged him to challenge himself but also held him back when he thought he was too young or not ready for the next step. When Neymar was fourteen years old and approached by Real Madrid, Neymar Pai resisted. He said, "We're from a humble family, and in a humble family there is always the question of cultural values. We thought he had to grow up in Brazil. That was the first serious choice we had to make." Neymar has always been very grateful for his father's attentiveness and business acumen. He has said, "I'm extremely lucky that I have more than a father; I have by my side, more than anything else, my best friend." Neymar's father is more than just his role model for soccer—he is his role model for life.

made with colored glass mosaics, copper domes, granite, and exotic hardwoods. Today, modern skyscrapers line the beaches, harbor, and downtown business center. There are numerous museums, galleries, theaters, shops, parks, restaurants, and nightclubs. Of course, not all of Santos is prosperous. Santos is also home to one of Brazil's largest *favelas*. Favelas are hillside neighborhoods home to extremely poor people living in poorly built shacks, most with no electricity, running water, or sanitation.

However, for Neymar, the Santos he came to know was the glittering city. He was impressed with the bright lights and the hustle and bustle, and Santos was impressed with Neymar. The Santos team owners hired coaches who knew how to work with young players, or *meninos*. Just before Neymar joined the Santos academy, future stars such as Robson de Souza (known as Robinho) and Diego Ribas (known as Diego) helped Santos return to its former glory. The team won the Brazilian championship that year—a long thirty-four years after the Peixe's last victory. Santos FC knew they were on the right track. They were developing a new group of meninos, which included Neymar.

Soccer, Brazil Style

Coach Betinho taught his young players how to use traditional Brazilian dance moves to enhance their game. His method was to teach the young players a dance step called the *ginga* (pronounced jeen-gah) and a dance style called the samba. In the youth academy, players continued to play five-a-side futsal. With futsal, the coach explained, Brazilian kids had to be creative. They played in a confined space and needed to move quickly and creatively to score. There was no time to stand still with the ball. Betinho noticed that

To refine their skills, many Brazilian soccer players practice capoeira, a Brazilian martial art featuring dancing, twirling, and combat moves.

when he played samba music, the boys intuitively started to move their hips, spin, shimmy, and hop when they touched the ball.

Neymar was particularly skilled at ginga. Ginga is a basic part of the Brazilian martial art called capoeira. It came to Brazil by enslaved West Africans who were transported and forced to work on Portuguese sugar plantations, starting in the sixteenth century. Capoeira is made up of dance steps, twirls, leaps, and combat moves. Capoeira performers keep their arms and legs in constant motion to foil their opponents' attacks. They use their opponents' energy against them. Brazilian soccer players, especially Neymar, are known and respected for their unique and spirited style, which sometimes comes from practicing capoeira.

In Training

Players in the Santos youth academy were taught to play all positions in order to get the feel for how their opponents may move against them. They played as defenders, forwards, strikers, midfielders, and goalkeepers. They learned to kick with both their left and right foot. They focused on ball control, passing, and shooting. Importantly, they were taught teamwork. Soccer relies on the ability of players to act smoothly as a team.

Coaches have said that once on the pitch, Neymar could change the course of a game. However, he was good to his teammates and worked well with them. His friendliness prevented other players from feeling jealous. In youth soccer, there are levels of players according to age. Before becoming a professional player, Neymar played on under-11, under-13, and under-17 teams. The under-11s and under-13s played five-a-side futsal. The players all competed in local, regional, and national games and tournaments. Under-17 as well as under-20 players played eleven-a-side football and competed internationally in junior FIFA World Cup tournaments.

In one memorable under-11 match, Neymar and his best friend and teammate Bruno Ferreira Bonfim (known as Dentinho, which means "little tooth" in Portuguese) showed their sense of teamwork and scored three points between them. Neymar provided Dentinho with two on-target, cross-field passes, allowing Dentinho to score. Dentinho, in turn, set up Neymar's goal, which was the final goal for the trophy win. The team won their first title, the Copa Uniligas.

In the under-11s, Neymar continued to stand out. Coaches soon opted to move Neymar to the under-13 level. There, Neymar played exclusively with older children. Professional striker and former Santos youth academy teammate Léo Baptistão says of Neymar, "What he does now on the pitch, he was already doing at the age of eleven. Let's just say that the tactics for lots of matches were just to pass the ball to Neymar and let him get on with it." Neymar was already earning the reputation of superstar striker.

Eleven-a-Side

By the time Neymar was twelve, the under-15 Santos coach, Antônio Lima dos Santos, known as Lima, had been hearing a great deal about the talented Neymar, but he did not focus on Neymar's talent because the boy had only been playing five-a-side futsal. However, as praise for Neymar grew louder, Lima went to the futsal pitch and watched him in action. He was thoroughly impressed but concerned that Neymar would not be able to handle a sudden switch from five-a-side to eleven-a-side. The more he watched Neymar, though, the more he wanted him for his under-15 team. He finally spoke to Zito. Zito protested, saying that Neymar was too small and thin and not

Antônio Lima dos Santos, Neymar's former Santos coach, stands in Urbano Caldeira Stadium.

physically strong enough to play with older teenagers. The coaches compromised. Zito let Neymar train but not compete with the under-15s.

In practice, Lima played Neymar at midfield. Neymar was unhappy with the position. He wanted to be a winger or a striker—that is, the player who contributes most to the scoring by passing cross-field or shooting goals. However, Lima was firm. Neymar was not big enough nor strong enough to defend himself from the hardest-hitting defenders. As a midfielder, Lima insisted, Neymar would be playing in a different section of the pitch, away from the strongest defenders. Nevertheless, Lima said, Neymar would still be in a position to get the ball and strike. Lima and the other coaches knew they needed to protect Neymar from his own enthusiasm, as much as they wanted to encourage his determination. Defenders, especially those charged with protecting the goal, are usually large, bulky, and very strong physical players. Neymar was not only slim and small, but he was also younger. Being a winger or striker would have to wait, the coaches told Neymar.

Neymar was determined to play eleven-a-side ball. Although he was younger than his teammates, he surpassed most of them in training. He ran on the track, he worked out with weights, and he stayed longer at practice than any of the others. Nearly every night, he begged his coach to stay so he could practice extra free kicks.

Real Madrid

When Neymar was just twelve, Betinho introduced him and his family to Wagner Ribeiro, a sports agent. Ribeiro was impressed with Neymar to the degree that he provided Neymar's family with a monthly stipend. He planned to see to it that Neymar would be treated fairly in any contract he might sign.

News of Neymar's exceptional talent had spread to Europe. Coaches and management of the Real Madrid soccer club heard of Neymar. They contacted Ribeiro and asked him to bring Neymar to Spain. Although Neymar was only fourteen, he and Neymar Pai knew that playing in a European league was a big opportunity. In March 2006, Neymar, Neymar Pai, and Ribeiro flew to Madrid.

Brazilian-born Robinho, playing here for Real Madrid, has faced legal and personal problems in recent years but was an early soccer influence for Neymar.

Neymar was shy when he first arrived. Coaches did not know what to expect, but they were amazed by the way he dribbled, passed, and shot for goals. He was a natural. After two weeks of training, Neymar joined the rest of the team on the pitch for a friendly game. Coaches had never seen anyone at age fourteen play any better. The other players, rather than being jealous of Neymar, were excited to have him join their team.

Neymar was equally excited. Real Madrid was a powerful soccer club in a major European soccer league. The city in itself was exciting. However, the most thrilling experience for Neymar was meeting the famous Brazilian soccer players Robson de Souza (known as Robinho) and Romário de Souza Faria (known as Romário), who played for Real Madrid.

Neymar and his father felt that living in Spain would be an exciting change for the whole family. Ribeiro negotiated a contract with Real Madrid. It would provide Neymar and his family with a generous income. Neymar and Rafaella would be enrolled in private school. Their housing would be paid for as well. It was a dream coming true in just three short weeks. However, after those three weeks, Neymar started to have second thoughts. He missed Santos and his teammates, coaches, and friends. He missed his mother's cooking. Stunning everyone, Neymar and Neymar Pai flew back to Brazil. Waiting for them were the owners of Santos. They offered Neymar a better contract and a signing bonus, which Neymar signed. At age fifteen, Neymar earned nearly $3,000 per week. Santos also promised to give him more time on the pitch. The family was now able to afford a new apartment near Santos's stadium, Urbano Caldeira Stadium.

100% JESUS

Chapter 3

Jogo Bonito

Jogo Bonito has become a popular nickname for soccer. It means "Beautiful Game" in Portuguese. The beautiful game of soccer is played everywhere, and it can be played with any group of people, any kind of ball, and a couple of goal markers. Millions of people have grown up playing soccer and love the game. So, it is no wonder that professional soccer players have a special spot in the hearts of their fans. Stars, such as Neymar, are national heroes.

A Young Hero

In 2007, as Neymar continued his upward path, Real Madrid again tried to lure him to Spain. Neymar was not as tempted this time. He knew that if his professional career continued to be successful, he would sign with a European team. However, as a teenager, his loyalty remained with Santos, the Paulista league, and Brazil.

The São Paulo Youth Football Cup, nicknamed Copinha (meaning "Little Cup"), is the premier youth soccer tournament in

Opposite: Neymar attracts devoted fans every time he takes to the pitch.

Brazil. In January of 2008, Neymar was selected to be a member of the Santos team made up of players 20 years old and younger. There were eighty-eight teams. Neymar, at age fifteen, was expected to stay on the bench. He was the youngest player in the tournament. Fans, however, were calling out for him. Near the end of the second game, coaches relented and called Neymar to the pitch to give him a little experience. While Neymar did not score a goal in the game, he made three major assists, and the Santos under-20s won 5–1. In an interview after the game, Neymar promised that Santos was going to be a championship team very soon.

In 2009, Neymar advanced to the junior team and practiced with the first team. The first-team players made sure Neymar got a full dose of the rigors of professional ball. However, Neymar was not perturbed by their aggressive play. He wanted to join the first team and played fearlessly. The coach held him off, saying he wasn't strong enough yet. By the end of the year, though, the coach had resigned, and Neymar was on the first team. Neymar played his first professional game on March 7, 2009. He came on the pitch to a standing ovation. Eight days later, he scored his first goal. Playing against a Paulista rival, Neymar scored in the twenty-eighth minute of the second half. It was a diving header. After scoring, Neymar jumped up and pointed his index finger toward the sky, in imitation of Pelé and as an homage to his grandfather. Later in the season, as Santos entered the Paulista Cup, Neymar scored several goals and helped his team reach the semifinals. They lost in the final to Cristiano Ronaldo's team, the Corinthians, but Neymar was awarded the Best Young Player of 2009 trophy.

Neymar was selected to join the Brazilian under-17 team. They competed in Lagos, Nigeria, in the FIFA U-17 World Cup in the

Neymar, despite being one of the youngest players on the under-17 team, was a stand-out scorer.

fall of 2009. It was a huge honor. Brazil's first match was against Japan. In the sixty-seventh minute of the game, a teammate passed the ball to a waiting Neymar. His response was to flip the ball past the goalkeeper and then to move quickly in the opposite direction to kick the ball into the net. People said it reminded them of a memorable play by Pelé. Brazil's U-17 team won the match but did not advance very far in the tournament. However, it was Neymar's first appearance in front of the world, and he made his mark.

Neymar finished his first full professional season in 2010 with forty-two goals in sixty games. Santos finished first in the Paulista league and won the national tournament, the Copa da Brasil (the Brazil Cup). Neymar was the top scorer, with eleven goals. He was voted Best Player of the Year.

A Big Mistake

Despite Neymar's achievements in 2010, he was not yet a mature professional. His immaturity was very apparent in September of that year. In a match at Santos's home stadium, the team was down 0–2 in a game they should have been winning. At one point, Neymar was fouled. He set up to prepare for a penalty kick, but the coach sent another player to take the kick. Neymar got angry. His teammates tried to calm him down. His teammate scored. Nearly the same incident happened again in the game. This time, Neymar yelled at his coach. After his teammate's second penalty kick also led to a score, Neymar took hold of the ball and selfishly did not assist anyone. He dribbled up and down the pitch and eventually scored two goals. Although Santos won, 4–2, it was not a happy victory.

After the match ended, Neymar rushed to the locker room and argued more with his coach. The coach was also angry and felt that Neymar needed to learn a lesson. He suspended him for two games. The next match, played without Neymar, ended in a lackluster tie of 0–0. However, the match after that was against city rivals, the Corinthians. The fans wanted Neymar back. Santos's management felt that having a soccer icon on the team was more important than the coach. The coach was fired, and Neymar played. Neymar's parents were heartbroken over his behavior. At first, Neymar defended himself, tweeting that he was upset at not getting the penalty kicks because it would have been best for the team if he had. No one considered that much of an apology. Neymar's parents and teammates talked to him, and they encouraged him to verbally apologize.

After much soul-searching and thoughts of quitting the sport, Neymar apologized saying, "I apologize to all those who love Neymar and the kids who look up to me. I ask for forgiveness because what happened last night was not the Neymar people want to see. Neymar is happiness, football with a smile across his face." While his apology was sincere, this wouldn't be the last time that Neymar's temper would get the best of him.

A Banner Year

The year 2011 was one of extraordinary events for Neymar. By the end of 2010, Santos was the national champion. Neymar was their star. Soon, European teams came calling. This time it was two powerhouse teams from England—Chelsea and West Ham United.

They offered a lot of money, far more than Santos could possibly pay. Santos's owners did not have much time to decide whether they would try to prevent another team from buying out Neymar's contract. Santos's management acknowledged that the Brazil league

SEARA
BANCO
BMG

Playing for Santos, Neymar became a star as the top scorer.

was a less competitive organization than the British league. They were torn between wanting the best for Neymar and wanting to keep him. That year, Santos, with Neymar as the star, was in line to win the continental tournament, the Copa Libertadores de America.

A meeting was arranged between Neymar, Neymar Pai, Neymar's agent, and Santos's management. Neymar Pai and the agent were very interested in the offers and felt that Neymar was ready for the English Premier League (England's top soccer league). Neymar Pai wanted to see Neymar become one of the greatest stars in European soccer. The money would make the family rich beyond their wildest dreams. The Santos management saw their side was losing, until a telephone call came in. It was Pelé. One of the world's all-time great athletes wanted to talk to Neymar and his father.

Pelé told Neymar that he did not think he was mature enough to stand out in the European leagues. He felt Neymar needed to focus on developing his skills instead of spending his training time learning to adapt to the style of European soccer. Pelé told Neymar Pai that if Neymar were his son, he would not want him to leave Santos at this time. He reminded both that he had played his entire career with Santos and had nonetheless achieved worldwide acclaim. Neymar recalled later, "That decision would be a turning point in my life. Even Pelé called me. Can you imagine how important I felt? The King of Football called me and asked me to stay."

Contract talks stalled after that momentous phone call. Santos did not have the money to prevent Neymar from leaving, so the agent suggested the club help Neymar acquire product endorsements. Rather quickly, Nike, Panasonic, and Red Bull signed endorsement contracts with Neymar. Ten more sponsors later came forward. The sponsorships provided more than enough money to keep Neymar at Santos, for the time being.

At the 2011 FIFA celebration, Neymar holds his Puskás Award trophy, given to the player who had scored the year's most beautiful goal.

Santos went on to win the national title. In one series match, Santos lost to Flamengo 4–5. However, many watching the game called it historic. The teams were equally matched. Both Neymar and the leading scorer for Flamengo, nicknamed El Gaucho, were playing their best. Neymar's first goal was a stunner. He received the ball about midfield and attracted several defenders. He escaped and dribbled forward. He tapped the ball around the goalkeeper. The goalkeeper came off the line, and two defenders lunged forward. Neymar sent the ball over their heads and smashed it into the back of the net. That goal earned Neymar one of FIFA's most prestigious awards—the Puskás Award. The award is given for the year's most beautifully played goal. Two other players were nominated for the award—British top-scoring forward Wayne Rooney and the legendary Lionel Messi, who would one day be Neymar's teammate.

Following the national championship, Santos won the Copa Libertadores. Neymar scored the opening goal of the final game, and throughout the tournament, he scored six goals in thirteen appearances. Santos had not won the Copa Libertadores since Pelé was on the team in 1963. Neymar was voted Best Player of the Year. Winning the Copa Libertadores qualified Santos to play in the 2011 FIFA Club World Cup, which took place in December in Japan. The FIFA Club World Cup is a tournament between the winning clubs from each of the six continental confederations, plus the league winner of the host nation. Santos, representing South America, did brilliantly up until the final match. Neymar's future team, Barcelona, won the cup 4–0. Neymar was the third highest scorer in the tournament, with six goals; two other players scored seven goals. For his achievement, Neymar was awarded the "Bronze Boot."

In 2012, Neymar reached a milestone; he scored his 100th professional league goal. Most of the goals had been for Santos.

Statisticians have pointed out that of his first hundred goals, seventy were kicked by his right foot, twenty-one were by his left, seven goals were headers, and one each was scored with his shoulder and his chest. His 100th goal was a header.

In the 2012 Paulista tournament, Santos took home the top trophy, its third in a row. This had not been achieved since the 1960s when Pelé played on the team. In 2012, Neymar received two tournament awards—best goal scored and best striker.

Life Change

Neymar's 100th goal was an important milestone he hit at the beginning of the 2010s, but another was more personal than professional. In August 2011, Neymar and his girlfriend at the time, Carolina Dantas, welcomed a baby boy they named Davi Lucca. Although very young—Neymar was just nineteen and Carolina was seventeen—the two became very loving and attentive parents. The couple did not marry, but Neymar and Carolina are both devoted to their son.

The Olympics

Neymar was selected for the Brazilian national team that would be going to the 2012 London Olympics. Neymar was impressive at the 2012 Olympics. He was new on the world soccer scene, but he soon stood out to all who watched him—just as he had been doing all his life.

Sports reporters were excited, including Marc Jensen, who reported on Neymar's "dazzling footwork," "dashing creativity," "no fear attitude … and free-wheeling Brazilian offense." Spectators compared him to the greatest stars of the day, such as Cristiano Ronaldo and Lionel Messi. In the Olympics, Neymar scored three goals, including a thrilling game-winning penalty kick in the quarterfinals. Brazil was very competitive and played to the final match. They lost 2–1 in a rousing game against Mexico. No small feat, however, was it to bring home an Olympic silver medal. Despite the loss, Neymar was joyful and optimistic. Brazil would win gold the next time, he promised.

Barcelona

How did Barcelona win Neymar? Besides having the money to buy out Neymar's Santos contract, Barcelona also touched Neymar emotionally. His decision-making had its start at the 2011 FIFA Club World Cup in Japan. Playing against Barcelona, Neymar at times was brilliant. However, he and Santos fell far short of Barcelona's performance. Neymar's uniquely clever and dance-like moves were no match for the hard-hitting Barcelona defenders. However, Barcelona played a more free-spirited game than other European teams. Barcelona controlled the ball for more than seventy out of the ninety minutes of play. After the 4–0 trouncing, Neymar realized he had a lot to learn about playing European soccer. He was humbled but determined.

Neymar and everyone around him knew that he would eventually join a European club. It became apparent in 2013 that Neymar would probably break his contract with Santos before its 2014 expiration date. English teams came calling, as well as Real Madrid and Barcelona. In many interviews, Neymar said he was happy staying with Santos and he felt he was still too young to leave. However, that would not turn out to be so.

When he was ready to choose between competing clubs, Neymar remembered the night in 2011 when Santos had been so badly beaten by Barcelona. His words then were, "What Barcelona did today was amazing. They were far, far the better team and we learned how to play football today. I've grown up watching this side [team] play and learning from them, but you take in so much more out on the pitch. I'm going to look on this game as a lesson."

After officially announcing that he would be joining Barcelona, he was taken by helicopter to a beach resort. It did not sit well with Santos fans. In leaving, Neymar scrawled a message in the locker room for his teammates, "I am leaving but I will be back." To his multitude of fans, Neymar went on Facebook and wrote:

> I want to thank all the Santos fans for these nine incredible years. My feelings for the club and the fans will never die. They are eternal! Only a club like Santos could give me all that I have had both on and off the pitch. I am grateful to the Peixe fans who have supported me, even in hard times. Titles, goals, dribbling, celebrations and songs that the fans have created for me will be with me forever in my heart.

During his five years on Santos's first team, Neymar played 229 games and scored 138 goals. It came to an end on May 26, 2013, when Neymar played his last match as a Santos forward. It was a match against Flamengo in the national tournament. Nearly 64,000 spectators came to the stadium. Unfortunately, the spectators did not get much of a show. Many Santos fans booed Neymar and flung insults at him. Neymar did not score, and the game ended in a 0–0

Neymar versus Lionel Messi

Neymar was a soccer prodigy from an early age. For most of his career, other players showed little jealousy. Even as a young boy playing in the streets, children wanted him to play with them. In school, his teammates and classmates liked his friendly ways and admired his enormous talent. When Neymar played in futsal leagues, his teammates did not begrudge him his skill or popularity. Given such, Neymar did not know a true rival. Even today, any talk of rivalry comes mostly from fans and observers. In this regard, most would say that Lionel Messi is his foremost rival.

Messi is an Argentinian. Brazil and Argentina have been confederation rivals for more than one hundred years. Messi is Argentina's star and captain, and Neymar was Brazil's captain for a time. The teams are equally matched; both are ranked in the top ten of teams in the world. They share about the same number of international trophies. When Neymar was turning Santos into a top-tier team, Messi was already a superstar in Barcelona. Coming to Barcelona in 2013, Neymar joined Messi and forward Luis Suárez to form an inimitable trio of playmakers. Although they supported each other as teammates, Messi has surpassed Neymar in one important category—the FIFA Ballon d'Or (meaning "Golden Ball" in French), which is given to the best soccer player in the world. By 2019, Messi had won his fifth Ballon d'Or, and Neymar had won none. When Neymar suddenly left Barcelona for Paris, observers said he wanted to get out from under Messi's shadow. He wanted to win the FIFA Ballon d'Or.

Playing for Brazil in the 2018 World Cup, Neymar dribbles past Argentina's Lionel Messi, his former Barcelona teammate.

tie. However, Neymar had led Santos through its best winning streak since the reign of Pelé.

Golden Ball

After signing with Barcelona, Neymar was excited and emotional. He talked about living his dream and having the opportunity to play with "some of the best players in the world." However, he was back in Brazil soon after departing to play in the 2013 FIFA Confederations Cup. The tournament was being held in Brazil, just like the 2014 FIFA World Cup tournament. Like Neymar, many soccer superstars play in the European confederation, which includes leagues from twenty-four European countries, but most return home to play for their national teams in the World Cup, Confederations Cup, and Olympics.

The 2013 FIFA Confederations Cup was played in the Brazilian capital of Brasilia. The event was enthusiastically anticipated by Neymar's fans. After a thrilling opening ceremony, Brazil came onto the pitch to play against Japan. Within minutes, Neymar scored. It was a difficult and beautiful play and a fitting one to begin the tournament. Playing off a bouncing chest pass, Neymar half-volleyed the ball into the net. The screams from the Brazilian fans were thunderous. Neymar looked to the sky and was mobbed by his teammates. He scored again at the start of the second half. The match ended as a 3–0 victory for Brazil. Neymar's former Santos coach, Muricy Ramalho, believed that Neymar had played so extraordinarily well because he was home and no longer had the weight of indecision on his shoulders.

Brazil, led by Neymar, powered its way to the final match against World Cup and European champions Spain. The game

Neymar holds up the 2013 FIFA Confederations Cup, which Brazil won 3–0 over Spain.

felt momentous. The national anthem was played; the crowd was ecstatic. In the opening minutes, Brazil forward Frederico Chaves Guedes (known as Fred) fell to the pitch but managed to scoop his foot under the ball and send the ball into the net. Spain was shocked, and the Brazilian crowd roared. Spain's deficit increased later in the half, when Neymar received a pass and sent a powerful left-footed shot into the roof of the net. The fans were so raucous the game had to pause. Both Fred and Neymar jumped the side fences and were mobbed by an adoring crowd of fans. Fred scored again in the second half, and the match ended with a score of 3–0 Brazil. The stadium erupted. The Brazilian team had ended Spain's world-record run of unbeaten games and had won the 2013 Confederations Cup. Neymar was awarded the FIFA Confederations Cup Bronze Boot and Golden Ball for being the "Man of the Match." Much was forgiven by Neymar's fans as they looked forward to seeing him return the following year for the 2014 World Cup in Brazil.

2014 World Cup

Brazil hosted the 2014 World Cup. Again, Brazil's fans were eager to cheer for their homegrown superstar. Coming off Brazil's glorious victory the year before, excitement was in the air. The world was watching. The sportswear company Nike weighed in with an advertising campaign called "Dare to be Brazilian."

Brazil won its first match against Croatia and tied Mexico 0–0 in the second. Brazil's third match, against Cameroon, carried a lot of drama. Neymar scored the 100th goal of the tournament in fine "Neymar" fashion. His teammate Luiz Gustavo passed to Neymar, who spread his body wide and side kicked the ball into the corner. Neymar scored again later for his fourth goal of the tournament. In the middle of the second half, however, Neymar was fouled and left the pitch with a sore knee. Brazil carried on and won the match 4–1. Neymar was named Man of the Match.

The next match, against Chile, was a nail-biter. It ended in a 1–1 tie to be decided by penalty kicks, which Brazil won, 3–2. The next match, against Colombia, led to Brazil's unexpected downfall. Although Brazil won the match, 2–1, the game ended in despair. Brazil's leading defender, Thiago Silva, was given a red card (a card shown by the referee that means a player has broken the rules and will not be allowed to continue playing) and suspended. The worst imaginable luck continued when the Colombian defender Juan Zuniga kneed Neymar in the back. Neymar crashed to the ground, writhing in pain. Neymar has often been accused of diving and overdramatizing fouls, but this time was real. Doctors came on the field. Neymar insisted he wanted to continue to play. However, to his and everyone's horror, he could not move his legs. He had broken a vertebra in his back and was carried off the pitch. Fans looked on with disbelief. As fans held up Neymar jerseys and banners, Brazil returned to finish the match. By winning, they moved on to the quarterfinals against Germany.

In the match against Germany, Brazil suffered an embarrassing defeat. Without their star forward, they lost to Germany with a shocking score of 7–1. Brazil later lost the match for third place to the Netherlands 3–0. Brazil was demoralized. Not in recent memory had Brazil given up ten goals in a row. Brazil's coaches and fans were furious over Neymar's injury. The defender, Zuniga, was never penalized for his foul.

Neymar was sidelined for three months. However, he eventually returned to play for Barcelona. With typical bravado, he declared

Defenders from opposing teams frequently target and foul Neymar.

that he was ready to take on Germany and looked forward to playing for Brazil in the 2018 World Cup.

LEMINA
18
Cygames

Chapter 4

Winning Seasons

Neymar became a major force behind Barcelona's growing success. Although he had joined a team already filled with exceptional talent, Neymar tipped the scales. On July 30, 2013, Neymar came onto the pitch for his new team, Barcelona, in a friendly match in Thailand. He played his first competitive match for Barcelona the following month. From there, he rose to glory.

La Liga

Barcelona is one of the premier European soccer teams. Officially known as Futbol Club Barcelona, or FC Barcelona, the team is also nicknamed Barça. The club belongs to La Liga Nacional de Fútbol Profesional (National Professional Soccer League), commonly called La Liga. Twenty of the top Spanish teams play in La Liga, including Barcelona's chief rival, Real Madrid. La Liga is the upper-level division of the Royal Spanish Football Federation (in Spanish it is called Real Federación Española de Fútbol, abbreviated

Opposite: Neymar, playing for Barcelona, kicks the ball between the legs of Mario Lemina (#18) of Juventus in an International Champions Cup match.

RFEF). RFEF belongs to the confederation of European soccer organizations called the UEFA (Union of European Football Associations). There are twenty-four countries that belong to UEFA. Within the UEFA is an upper-level division called the Champions League. The Champions League is the top league in Europe. Each of these organizations sponsors competitions and awards trophies and honors.

Good Times and Bad Times

In August 2013, Neymar played with Barcelona in a friendly match in Bangkok, Thailand. Early in the game, Messi gave Neymar an assist, and Neymar easily tapped the ball in to score. On August 17, he played his first official professional match. He entered the game late as a substitute in a game that was already won (Barcelona 7–0). On August 21, 2013, in competition for the Spanish Super Cup, Neymar again came in late in the game as a substitute. Within seven minutes, he had scored his first goal. Barcelona came away from the match with the Spanish Super Cup trophy.

Barcelona competed in the 2013 Champions League tournament, the most prestigious tournament in Europe. In one match, Neymar scored three goals, which is called a hat trick, in just fourteen minutes in front of a delighted Barcelona crowd. Barcelona won, 6–1.

The 2014 season did not begin well. First, Messi was injured. When Messi returned, he and Neymar played just a few games together, and then Neymar injured his ankle and was out for a month. Neymar and his father were undergoing legal battles in the courts over payments made by Barcelona to Santos, and Neymar grew distracted. Messi and Neymar were not able to create any chemistry between them.

Neymar took a break from Barça to play for the Brazilian national team in South Africa. There, he played well and enjoyed the familiar cheers from a loving Brazilian crowd. However, when he returned to Barcelona, the team was still out of sync. They fell out of the UEFA Champions League tournament as well as the Copa del Rey (the RFEF Cup). For the first time in several years, Barcelona finished its season without winning a trophy. Neymar had suffered—from injuries, legal battles, homesickness, and a feeling of not fitting in in Europe. It was not a good year for Neymar professionally or personally. Barça players were resentful that he was making more money than most everyone else on the team. He was often taunted by Barça fans while playing and produced only fourteen goals and eight assists in fifty-three matches.

The Trident

Fortunately, the season from 2014 to 2015 was not only better, but it also was one of the best seasons the team ever had. Barcelona— with Neymar, Messi, and Uruguayan Luis Suárez aboard—achieved a treble, and Barcelona is the only team to have done so twice (2008–2009 was the other treble season). The treble refers to winning the three major European trophies—the La Liga championship, the Copa del Rey, and the UEFA Champions League trophy. Besides the treble, Barça also won the 2015 FIFA Club World Cup against the Argentine club River Plate, 3–0. Neymar recalled his painful experience at the 2011 FIFA Club World Cup. Santos's sudden fall from grace at the hands of Messi and the Barcelona club had been a shock. After the 2015 Barcelona win,

Neymar said, "Today, I'm on the other side of the fence, and I'm glad about that. I'm very happy to be a world champion." Neymar regained his confidence.

The 2015 season saw Messi, Neymar, and Suárez play with a sharp three-pronged attack against their opponents. Fans called the trio "the Trident." That year, the Trident scored an impressive 122 goals between them. They were the highest-scoring threesome in Spanish soccer history. In the following season, they bested themselves with an amazing 131 goals. Not only were they effective, but they also acted as true teammates, sharing goals, passes, and assists. Neymar said, "Even though we have a very strong rivalry on the national teams—Brazil, Argentina, and Uruguay—we get along really well. I'm really proud to be part of this trident and proud that we are making soccer history. We don't want to stop now, we want to keep writing history." They continued to do just that.

Neymar and Messi were recognized as the team leaders. When Messi was out for ten games due to injury, Neymar took over. He scored eleven goals out of the twenty-seven scored during Messi's time away. When Messi returned, Neymar graciously relinquished the top position.

By the end of the season, Neymar was the team's second highest scorer, after Messi. He had forty-three goals in forty-seven professional matches. He was the top scorer in the Copa del Rey with eleven goals, and won the Man of the Match trophy. He also tied Messi and Real Madrid forward Cristiano Ronaldo with ten goals each in the Champions League tournament. In the thrilling final match for the UEFA Champions League trophy, Neymar scored the final and winning goal and won against the Italian club Juventus, 3–1. On winning the Champions League, Neymar said, "I have

In this locker room photo, the uniforms and boots of Barcelona stars Neymar, Messi, and Suárez are lined up.

played many finals but I think this is the most important match of my life." Neymar was excited to be playing his best and winning.

Footwork

Neymar brought his fleet-footed, balletic style to Barcelona. Neymar's key talent is that he is a superlative dribbler. In an article in the *New York Times* about Neymar's ball handling, reporter Sam Borden wrote, "He can flick it, roll it, slide it, and cradle it. He can

FOULQUIER
2

Neymar has shown his skills playing for many teams, including Barcelona and Paris Saint-Germain (shown here).

make it disappear." Neymar is credited for being one of the best at nutmegging opponents. (A nutmeg is when a player kicks the ball between the legs of a defender and then continues to have possession of the ball once it has gone through.) Moreover, Neymar always seems to know what will happen next, like a grandmaster chess player.

Playing for Santos, Neymar was inspired by Brazilian dance and the Brazilian martial art capoeira. His soccer skills resemble that of Pelé's and other Brazilian greats. The style, often called *futbol arte* (football art), is theatrical, improvisational, and rhythmic. The style of Spanish soccer, especially perfected by Barcelona, is called *tiki-taka* (a Basque expression for taking quick, light steps). Tiki-taka is known for fast passing between two or three players until an opening to score is found. Neymar, Messi, and Suárez worked exceptionally well together to master the technique. However, most say Neymar's true talents are best seen in his capoeira-influenced dribbling.

Yellow Cards

After winning against a La Liga rival, Barcelona coach Luis Enrique praised his new player saying, "Neymar is electric, and at the moment, defenders only have two choices when facing him: commit a penalty or let him score. In one word, he was breathtaking." By soccer standards, Neymar is thin. His body type works for him and against him. He is incredibly agile due to his size, but that also makes him vulnerable to attacks by defenders. Given his talent, most observers admit that he is unfairly targeted. Numerous times, he has been intentionally kicked. Defenders do not seem to get yellow cards (warnings) as often as his team feels they should, and Neymar is not given as many free kicks as they believe he deserves. In many instances, Neymar has left the pitch injured because of a foul.

Neymar is known for—and his detractors call him out for—being overly theatrical on the pitch. His detractors say he dives to the ground at the merest suggestion of a foul. When a foul is not called, he often writhes in agony. Critics say he is just trying to get a free kick. In his defense, Neymar, his coaches, and his supporters say his South American style of drama on the pitch is a means of telling hard-hitting defenders to back off. His Brazilian team coach Luiz Scolari said, "He gets fouled ten times a match … The coaches who criticize Neymar, who claim he falls over or simulates fouls, do that because it's an easy way out for them … whenever somebody is really good, when you have players who can improvise and create things, it causes bad feelings." In an interview, Neymar commented on his style of playing soccer:

> I am not going to change, of course I won't change. People have to know that when you go on the pitch I have my way of playing and my way of playing is this, to dribble, to score goals, to help my teammates and I'm happy playing this way … In football you give elbows and kicks, but not everyone can dribble. I won't change my way of playing.

Neymar's supporters say that he cannot be faulted for wanting to protect himself. He also cannot be faulted for wanting to seek vengeance. However, Neymar's style of vengeance is not to hurt anyone, but rather to outdance, outdribble, and outsmart his opponents.

Going for Gold

Following the successful season from 2015 to 2016 with Barcelona, Neymar wanted to return and play for Brazil's national team. His Barcelona coaches did not want to spare him. They gave him a choice: He could play for Brazil in the Copa América Centenario, the 100-year anniversary of the South American soccer trophy, which that year would also include North and Central America, or he could play for Brazil in the Summer Olympics. Difficult as the choice was, Neymar chose the Olympics. The final matches of the 2016 Olympics were held in Rio de Janeiro, Brazil. Not only were the Olympics to be played on home soil for the Brazilian team, but Olympic gold was the one achievement Brazil had yet to realize. Brazil had won five FIFA World Cups, three Olympic silver medals, and two Olympic bronze medals—but no gold. Neymar reflected on the opportunity to play in the Olympic Games saying,

> I'm picturing myself playing at the Games on home soil. It's a dream come true. I've played in the Confederations Cup and the World Cup in Brazil, and all that's missing for me are the Games. It's going to make me so happy. The Olympic Games are different because they include all the sports. The whole world, friends and family, come together to watch them.

No fan of Brazil's national team will forget the devasting upset loss to Mexico in the 2012 Olympics. So with great anticipation, raucous Olympics crowds filled the stands in 2016. They waved flags with the Brazil team's kit (uniform) colors—yellow, green, and blue.

Many wore jerseys that said "Neymar Jr." and his number—10, the same number Pelé wore.

Brazil's first two matches were 0–0 ties with South Africa and Iraq. Many became discouraged, including the team. However, Brazil's fans upped their support and cheered louder for their home team. The players believed that helped kick-start Brazil's play. In the final game of their group round, Brazil bested Denmark 4–0. In the next match, the quarterfinal, Neymar led his team to a 2–0 defeat of Colombia. His winning free kick soared over the head of the goalie and into the upper corner of the net.

Brazil played in the semifinals against Honduras in the main stadium in Rio: Maracanã Stadium. There, more than seventy thousand soccer fans filled the stands, most screaming for Brazil. For the team, said winger Gabriel Jesus, competing in Maracanã Stadium was "the dream of every Brazilian player." After Honduras won the kickoff, the midfielders shuffled the ball for a bit. Suddenly, Neymar came driving down on the Honduran defender who had the ball. The player panicked and kicked the ball toward midfield. Neymar stole the ball, the Honduran goalie jumped off the line, and Neymar tapped the ball in for a goal. In all, it took fifteen seconds to score. Neymar's goal was the fastest goal in Olympic history at that time.

Not only were fans in the stadium stunned, but so were the players, most of all Neymar, who needed to take a moment to realize he had already scored. The ensuing noise and confusion meant that the game had to be stopped for four whole minutes. Once the game restarted, it was all Brazil. Neymar was targeted and fouled nine times and carried off the field on a stretcher once. He returned quickly, though, and continued making brilliant plays, including scoring the final goal. The 6–0 victory carried Brazil to the Olympic finals to face Germany.

No Brazilian needed to be reminded of the devastating 7–1 loss Germany delivered them in the 2014 World Cup. Brazil was without the injured Neymar in that match. However, Neymar and his new, young, and energized Brazilian team were ready to take on Germany. Brazil, led by its famous team captain—Neymar—was determined to win Olympic gold.

The match with Germany was tense. The teams were evenly matched. Neymar scored first with a perfect free kick from 27 yards (24.7 meters). The crowd bellowed, "Olé, Olé, Olé!" In the second half, however, Germany tied the game. At ninety minutes, the game was tied. With extra time added, the tie was still unbroken. The win would have to come from a penalty shootout. The first four penalty kicks from each team were perfect. On the fifth kick for Germany, forward Nils Petersen missed the goal, blocked by Brazil's goalkeeper, Weverton da Silva.

The game to decide the Olympic gold medal would come down to the last penalty shot. That shot was Neymar's. Neymar said later, "I am remembering that walk. It was the most nervous moment of my life. I couldn't think of anything but 'For the love of God, where will I kick this ball?'" However, he looked completely calm as he stepped to the box. The crowd went eerily quiet. He picked up the ball and kissed it before placing it on the ground and positioning himself. He ran toward the ball and stuttered slightly, stepping sideways back-and-forth as if to stop, before kicking the ball. It flew into the top right corner of the net. The German goalkeeper misread Neymar's direction and defended the goal to the left. Neymar sunk to the ground with a groan and wept for joy. The

Neymar and his teammates show off their gold medals won at the 2016 Olympics in Brazil.

volume of noise in and around the stadium was earth-shattering. Fireworks exploded overhead. Outside, car horns blared and sirens went off. Fans danced, chanted, and sang. "That's it, we made history," said Neymar tearfully, "I don't have words to say anything. I can't describe my feelings right now. I just want to thank my

Praise for Neymar

"Neymar is a player with exceptional characteristics. He's magical."

—Gerard Pique, Barcelona defender

"He can be whatever he wants to be—everything is open for him. He's quick, skillful and excels one-on-one. He has everything."

—Lionel Messi, Barcelona striker

"His rise has not surprised me at all. Even when he was a kid his ability was obvious. Now he has reached the level of the best in the world."

—Ronaldinho, Brazil and Barcelona midfielder,
2005 FIFA World Player of the Year

"That he's a player who can unlock a game—like he did once again today—is something we already knew. But the most important thing is that he really wanted this fresh chance, having come so close to gold last time. Neymar is like that, he's a fighter, and that's why he gets the rewards. He deserves everything that he achieves in his life."

—Rogerio Micale, Brazil national team coach

"His talent aside, he's an incredible guy ... He looked out for people, he helped in difficult moments and lifted our heads back up. He told us that if we were patient enough, we'd fight back and this moment would come. We owe a large part of this triumph to him."

—Felipe Anderson, Brazil midfielder

"Any football fan has to appreciate what Neymar does, which sometimes seems more like ballet than dribbling. It's beautiful, it's effective and it's spectacular."

—Luis Enrique, Spanish national team manager

Paris Saint-Germain fans reach out to Neymar during a photo shoot.

teammates, my friends and my family, who have been by my side during the most difficult moments. It wasn't easy. I don't know what else to say, I'm just really happy." Neymar's teammates surrounded him and huddled together, sobbing, hugging and leaping in the air.

Paris Saint-Germain

Neymar had played for Barcelona for four years. By April 2017, he had scored one hundred goals for the team. As the Trident, he, Messi, and Suárez achieved an extraordinary feat. They had scored a combined total of 364 goals in 450 games. Neymar had made the most assists to his fellow forwards.

On April 7, Barcelona played a memorable quarterfinal game against Paris Saint-Germain (PSG). It was a 6–1 come-from-behind win. Neymar scored two of the goals. Soon after, though, on August 3, 2017, Neymar signed a contract with PSG. At his announcement, Neymar said, "I made a trio with Messi and Suárez that made history, conquered everything an athlete can conquer, lived unforgettable moments, lived in a city that is more than a city, it is a homeland." To which Messi tweeted, "It was an enormous pleasure to have shared all these years with you friend @neymarjr I wish you luck in this new stage of your life. See you. I love you." The beautiful game transformed their rivalry into a friendship.

NEYMAR JR
10

Chapter 5

Legend in His Own Time

Neymar accepted the offer to play for Paris Saint-Germain before his contract with Barcelona had ended. His choice was very controversial. As per Neymar's contract with Barcelona, any team wishing to sign Neymar needed to pay an unheard-of sum of $255 million. The price to buy out his contract was nearly double what it would cost for any other player's contract. Beyond that, Neymar would be paid $565,000 a week, making him the most expensive soccer player in the world. Many accused Neymar of leaving Barcelona for money. Others believed that Neymar was chasing his first Ballon d'Or, a trophy he would otherwise not likely achieve as long as he played alongside Lionel Messi.

Neymar countered his critics. He insisted that it was an honor to play with Messi and that leaving the team and his world-renowned teammate was not a matter of getting out from under Messi's shadow. Neymar had confidence in himself that he was a world-class player and was not outshone by a legend. He explained his choice to move on saying, "The life of an athlete is made by challenges. Some

Opposite: After signing a record-setting contract, Neymar stands with the president of Paris Saint-Germain and displays his new jersey.

are given to us, others are fruits of our own decisions—to keep the light that illuminates our career, which is intense, but short." His light would only get brighter.

In August 2017, Neymar played his first game at his new home. The Eiffel Tower in Paris was lit up to welcome him. He did not disappoint his new fans. Against French league rivals Toulouse, PSG won 6–2. Neymar scored two goals, the last coming just at the ninety-minute mark. French midfielder Lucas Deaux said, "I have never seen a player like this before." Just as he was with Santos, the Brazilian national team, and Barcelona, Neymar appeared to be friendly, respectful, and well-liked when he first arrived at PSG. Kylian Mbappé, another PSG star forward, said, "People see him doing tricks and dribbles and think he is only trying to enjoy himself, that he's selfish and only thinks about himself. But when you share a dressing room with him you realize that it's not the case. He's a very kind person, he is interested in others." Neymar's teammates see a very different side to Neymar. They see him as a team player who loves the game and respects his team.

PSG

Why did Paris Saint-Germain spend so much on Neymar? The last time PSG had won a continental trophy was the UEFA Cup Winners' Cup tournament in the season from 1992 to 1993. (The tournament no longer exists.) While PSG has frequently won the Ligue 1 trophy, Coupe de la Ligue (known in English as the French League Cup), and the Coupe de France (the French Cup), Paris Saint-Germain has never won the UEFA Champions League Cup. Neymar, the team owners believed, could be the answer.

After signing with PSG, Neymar said, "I came to Paris to be the best player in the world and to turn PSG into the best club in the world, which includes a Champions League trophy. We're ready and fear no one." In his first season, he scored twenty-eight goals in only thirty games. In the season from 2017 to 2018, PSG went on to win four French titles—Ligue 1, Coupe de France, the Coupe de la Ligue, and the French Championship trophy.

Neymar was becoming a leader on his team, but, unfortunately, he was also a target. In January 2018, he scored a whopping four goals and two assists in a Ligue 1 match against Dijon. Playing at that level invited defenders to go on the attack. Neymar was fouled eighty-eight times that season. In a match in early 2019, Neymar was kicked three times and left the pitch on a stretcher and in tears. He sustained a broken foot, and his recovery would force him to miss an important Champions League match with Manchester United. With Neymar in the stands, Paris Saint-Germain suffered a shocking loss in that match and was knocked out of the tournament. Everyone felt the pain of the loss of Neymar.

That pain for PSG continued into summer 2019, as rumors began to swirl that Neymar wanted to leave PSG. These rumors followed a difficult time for Neymar as a player and person. He was suspended from games for possible altercations with fans and insulting officials. In addition, PSG disciplined him after he missed training sessions. Neymar also faced personal and legal difficulties in summer 2019, as investigations began into an alleged sexual assault in his hotel room earlier that year. Neymar vehemently denied the allegations soon after they were first made, but investigations continued throughout the summer.

Neymar is known for his flashy style, tattoos, and hairstyles, in addition to his soccer skills.

Style and Swagger

Neymar is often in the news for more than just soccer. One of the more lighthearted things the media sometimes focuses on is his hair. He has sported one wild hairstyle after another. Back in 2010, Neymar and another Santos teammate cut their hair into Mohawks. Neymar Pai was not pleased until he saw how much the fans loved it. Young men throughout the country began wearing Mohawks. Neymar Pai joked, "In Brazil, only the president doesn't have a Mohawk." Since then, Neymar's hair has been dyed, bleached, shaven, permed, and moussed.

Neymar also has multiple tattoos, including the name of his son, Davi Lucca, on his leg and a portrait of his sister on his arm. He has an image of the Champions League trophy, which was added before Barcelona won. Neymar is also said to be very religious. He has a tattoo with an image of praying hands as well as the words, "Blessed," and "God is faith." On his shoulder is a prayer that Neymar says with his father before every soccer match. Across Neymar's upper back are the words, "*Ousadia e Alegria*," which means "boldness and joy" in Portuguese.

One of his newest tattoos is a drawing of a small boy holding a soccer ball in front of a favela, which is a slum, or poorer neighborhood in Brazil. The tattoo is to remind him of the poor neighborhood he grew up in.

Besides ever-changing hairstyles and tattoos, Neymar is a flashy dresser and indulges himself in luxuries. He owns several high-end cars, including a Ferrari, a Maserati, and a Porsche. He also has a private jet and a luxury yacht.

Neymar arrives in São Paulo to attend a charity auction to support a cause close to his heart,

Neymar is also a social media star. He has more than eighty million Instagram followers, sixty million Facebook followers, and thirty million Twitter followers. Unlike many celebrities, Neymar writes his own social media posts. Followers and fans feel like he is speaking directly to them. International corporations clamor for him to endorse their products. He is also one of the three highest-paid soccer players in the world and one of the most sought-after athletes for product sponsorships.

Free Time

For all the time that Neymar spends outdoors training and playing soccer, he prefers being indoors when he wants to relax and enjoy himself. He enjoys social media, online games, and video games, especially *FIFA*. He loves music and is a great dancer. One of his favorite pastimes is playing cards. A couple of times a year, Neymar invites his celebrity friends over for a charity game of poker. They have raised hundreds of thousands of dollars to feed those who live in poverty.

Beyond the Celebrity Life

Neymar is a celebrity whose dramatic personality has sometimes been a problem on and off the pitch. However, he is also said to be devoted to his parents, son, and sister. In addition, he is known for helping young people through various charitable efforts.

One touching moment occurred in Johannesburg, South Africa. Neymar had made a hat trick in a friendly match. After Brazil won, with people pushing toward the pitch to celebrate, a little boy ran onto the field. Security guards surrounded him, but Neymar picked up the little boy and carried him around on his shoulders.

Neymar poses next to the wood sculpture *Broken Chair* in Geneva, Switzerland, after being named goodwill ambassador for Handicap International.

NDICAP
RNATIONAL

He posed for pictures with the boy and included him in the team's celebrations.

Neymar has developed programs and supported causes to help the less fortunate. In August 2017, the United Nations named Neymar ambassador to Handicap International, believing his fame would lend a boost to their cause. The program's mission is to help vulnerable people who live with a disability in the world's poorest countries or who are victims of violent conflicts or natural disasters. An important program within the organization works to provide prosthetics to people with amputations, especially children. In his acceptance speech to the United Nations Neymar said, "I would like to begin by thanking you all for what you do for the least visible in the world." This is only one of many organizations that Neymar supports.

Neymar is also a spokesperson for a program called Teaching Kids. The program reaches out online to children with disabilities. The children in the program make videos that teach other people how to do something. Neymar was the first student in this program. Neymar said, "Thirty-two million disabled kids don't have access to school, yet they have so much to teach us." He watched while a blind girl taught him how to make an origami heart and a young boy with an amputated leg taught him a new dance.

Neymar is the founder of the Instituto Projeto Neymar Jr., a nonprofit organization dedicated to helping children, teenagers, and their families living in poverty. The institute is a school and sports complex located in Jardim Gloria, a community near where Neymar grew up.

The institute covers more than 90,417 square feet (8,400 square m) with a soccer pitch, swimming pool, gym, auditorium, and classrooms. Instituto Projeto Neymar Jr. presently provides 2,400 disadvantaged young people with an education, cultural activities, and sports training, with plans to support more than 10,000 young people and their families in the future.

The institute had always been a dream of both Neymar Pai and Neymar Jr. Neymar Pai said, "We want to pay forward all of the support that Neymar Jr. received in his training as an athlete. In order to become a high-performing player, Neymar Jr. had the support of many dedicated people."

The institute's mission statement says in part that it will "contribute to socially disadvantaged families' socio-educational development through sport." When the institute opened in 2014, a resident of the neighborhood, Gilberto Lael, said, "Let's hope that it brings many good things to this area. Jardim Gloria is not a favela but almost. Life here is not easy, especially for young kids." Neymar Jr. visits the school whenever he is in Brazil. He said, "The love I get from the kids, the conversations we have … it gives me strength to return to keep running after more trophies. It makes me really happy to do something for these kids and their families." Neymar hopes that he can provide opportunities to other children to help them out of poverty.

Neymar also cares about the environment. In fact, he is active in several environmental causes, such as saving African wildlife from poachers, preserving the Amazon River and jungle, and promoting better sanitation and clean water for the people of Rio de Janeiro and São Paulo. Neymar said, "I think it is the duty of all Brazilians and every human being who admires the Amazon to take care of our forests. We need to give back to nature all that she has given us." He even teamed up with the World Wildlife Fund to help promote

Neymar Scorecard

Although young, Neymar's career has been long. He began playing competitively as a futsal player in São Paulo, Brazil, in his early teens. He played his first professional match when he had just turned seventeen on March 7, 2009.

Club Highlights: With Neymar, Santos won Campeonato Paulista (2010, 2011, 2012); Santos won Copa Libertadores, which was the first since 1963 (2011); Santos won Recopa Sudamericana (2012); Brazil won Olympic silver medal (2012); Barcelona won Spanish Super Cup (2013); Barcelona won Liga Trophy (2014/2015; 2015/2016); Barcelona won Copa del Rey (2014/2015; 2015/2016; 2016/2017); Barcelona won UEFA Champions League (2014/2015); Barcelona won FIFA Club World Cup (2015); Brazil won Olympic gold medal (2016); PSG won Ligue 1 (2017/2018); PSG won

Coupe de France (2017/2018); PSG won Coupe de la Ligue (2017/2018); PSG won Trophée des Champions (2017/2018).

Individual Awards: Won FIFA Puskás Award for the best goal of the year (2011); named World Soccer Young Player of the Year (2011); named Copa Libertadores Most Valuable Player (2011); won FIFA Club World Cup Bronze Ball (2011); named South American Footballer of the Year (2011, 2012); won Confederations Cup Golden Ball (2013); won Confederations Cup Bronze Shoe (2013); awarded FIFA World Cup Bronze Shoe (2014); named La Liga Best World Player (2014/2015); named PSG Man of the Match, with four goals and two assists (January 2018).

awareness of the importance of protecting nature, especially the Amazon.

Neymar partners with a global soccer school system called Neymar Sports. The goal is to build at least one hundred sports schools around the world that provide opportunities for young people to play soccer and other sports and learn the values that sports can teach—such as commitment, teamwork, and respect.

From a kid playing soccer barefoot on the streets to the heights of wealth and fame, Neymar has never forgotten where he came from. Neymar carries the lessons from his coaches and parents close to his heart.

Moreover, he carries his passion. Neymar has written, "The only thing I never turn off is my passion. I live and breathe football." His deep passion for the game and how it is reflected in his exceptional skills distinguish him from many of the greats playing today.

Timeline

February 5, 1992 Neymar is born in Mogi das Cruzes, Brazil.

June 1992 A near fatal car accident injures Neymar's father.

1996 Neymar's family moves to São Vicente to live with his grandparents.

March 11, 1996 Neymar's sister, Rafaella, is born.

2002 Neymar begins futsal training at Portuguesa Santista FC and accepts a scholarship to Liceu São Paulo.

2003 Neymar enters Santos FC Academy.

March 30, 2006 Neymar signs, but does not formalize, contract with Real Madrid.

April 2006 Neymar returns to Santos.

September 30, 2007 Neymar signs a five-year contract with Santos.

March 7, 2009 Neymar makes his debut as a professional.

August 2011 Neymar's son, Davi Lucca, is born.

January 2012 Neymar signs $55 million deal with Santos.

Summer 2012 Neymar scores three goals in the London Olympics, helping Brazil win the silver medal.

May 2013 Neymar signs with Barcelona.

June 1, 2013 Neymar scores four goals to help Brazil win the Confederations Cup against Spain.

2014 Neymar scores thirty-nine goals in league competitions, helping Barcelona win the Treble—La Liga, Copa del Rey, and Champions League.

July 5, 2014 Neymar is fouled, breaks vertebra in his back, and is out for the rest of the World Cup.

August 20, 2016 Neymar scores the winning penalty shot to win the gold medal at the Rio de Janeiro Olympics.

August 3, 2017 Neymar signs with Paris Saint-Germain, making this the most expensive player transfer in history.

February 27, 2018 Neymar is fouled and breaks a bone in his foot.

January 30, 2019 Neymar is fouled and reinjures foot, causing him to miss the Champions League tournament.

Glossary

assist A pass that ends in a goal.

Ballon d'Or French for "Golden Ball." An annual award that honors a soccer player who performed the best over the previous year. It was originally an award for players from Europe, but in 2007, it became a global prize, meaning professional players around the world became eligible to win it.

boot A soccer shoe.

dribble A method of advancing the ball on the soccer field where players control the soccer ball by keeping it close to their feet and kicking it lightly.

FIFA The acronym used for the international soccer federation, which is the governing body of soccer worldwide. The acronym FIFA is based on the French name Fédération Internationale de Football Association.

forward A player who plays nearest the opposing team's goal and is responsible for most of the scoring.

free kick A kick that is awarded in soccer when a foul is committed by the offending team outside the penalty area.

friendly An exhibition game that is played outside of a competition.

futsal A type of soccer usually played indoors on a smaller field with only five players on a side.

goalkeeper The player who stands in front of the goal and defends shots from the opponents. Goalkeepers wear a different color kit and are allowed to use their hands. Also called goalie or keeper.

hat trick An achievement in which one player scores three goals in a single game or match.

header A method players use to pass, control, or score by bouncing the ball off of their head.

kit The name used to refer to the uniforms that soccer players wear.

midfielder A player who plays mostly in the middle portion of the field. Midfielders have different roles depending on the team's formation. For instance, some assist forwards or help out on defense.

nutmeg A maneuver a player uses that includes kicking the ball between an opponent's legs, running around the opponent, and then continuing on with the ball.

penalty shot A kick awarded to a player who has been fouled. The ball is placed 12 yards (about 11 m) from the goal.

pitch A soccer playing field.

red card The most serious penalty in soccer. It is given for foul play, abusive language, violent conduct, and deliberately touching the ball with a hand to prevent a goal.

striker A forward with excellent ball-handling skills who focuses on attacking the opposing team's goal.

UEFA The acronym for the Union of European Football Associations, the governing body of twenty-four European soccer leagues.

winger A player who can be a forward, midfielder, or defender and plays on the left or right side of the field.

World Cup The premier international soccer competition held every four years.

yellow card A penalty card held up by the referee that is given for unsportsmanlike behavior and delaying the game or arguing with another player or referee.

Further Information

Books

Caioli, Luca. *Neymar: The Unstoppable Rise of Barcelona's Brazilian Superstar*. London, UK: Icon Books, 2019.

Callow, Nick. *Neymar: The Ultimate Fan Book*. London, UK: Carlton Books Limited, 2018.

Killon, Ann. *Champions of Men's Soccer*. New York, NY: Philomel Books, 2018.

Oldfield, Matt, and Tom Oldfield. *Neymar: From the Playground to the Pitch*. London, UK: Dino Books, 2018.

Trusdell, Brian. *Neymar: Soccer Superstar*. New York, NY: SportsZone, 2018.

Websites

FIFA

http://www.fifa.com
The website of the Fédération Internationale de Football Association (FIFA), the international governing body for soccer, contains information about teams, statistics, schedules, matches, and player profiles.

Neymar Jr.

www.neymarjr10.com
Neymar's official website includes videos, news of his personal life, business activities, training routines, travel, and thoughts and commentary about soccer and world affairs.

Olympics

https://www.olympic.org
The official website of the Olympics includes accounts of historical games, articles, interviews, present schedules, and athlete profiles.

Paris Saint-Germain

https://en.psg.fr
The English-language version of the Paris Saint-Germain Football Club website includes stories, profiles of the squad, schedules, matches, honors and awards, videos, and photographs.

UEFA Champions League

https://www.uefa.com/uefachampionsleague
The website of the UEFA Champions League contains information on matches, players, awards, schedules, photographs, and videos.

Videos

Neymar's YouTube Channel

www.youtube.com/user/neymarjr
Neymar's YouTube channel shows Neymar's everyday activities, such as traveling, training, and commenting on events of personal interest to him. An English translation is available.

The Olympic Channel

www.youtube.com/watch?v=-Jmjn_dJt_4
Watch Neymar score the winning penalty shot for the gold medal at the Rio de Janeiro 2016 Olympic Games.

Bibliography

Borden, Sam. "A Soccer Prodigy, at Home in Brazil." *New York Times*, July 10, 2012. https://www.nytimes.com/2012/07/10/sports/soccer/neymar-soccer-prodigy-is-at-home-in-brazil.html.

Caioli, Luca. *Neymar: The Unstoppable Rise of Barcelona's Brazilian Superstar*. London, UK: Icon Books, 2019.

Callow, Nick. *Neymar: The Ultimate Fan Book*. London, UK: Carlton Books Limited, 2018.

"Can Neymar Lead Brazil to Glory in the 2019 Copa America?" Neymar Jr.net. Accessed on March 19, 2019. http://www.neymarjr.net/2019/01/25/can-neymar-lead-brazil-to-glory-in-the-2019-copa-america/.

"FIFA." FIFA.com. Accessed on March 19, 2019. http://www.fifa.com.

"FIFA Confederations Cup Brazil 2013: Awards." FIFA.com. Accessed on March 19, 2019. https://www.fifa.com/confederationscup/archive/brazil2013/awards/index.html.

Fitzpatrick, Richard. "Neymar Sr. Is the Driving Force Behind His Son's Push for World Domination." Bleacher Report, August 8, 2017. https://bleacherreport.com/articles/2726217-neymar-sr-is-the-driving-force-behind-his-sons-push-for-world-domination.

Foer, Franklin. "The Annoying Genius Who Makes the World Cup Worth Watching." *The Atlantic*, July 9, 2018. https://www.theatlantic.com/entertainment/archive/2018/07/he-annoying-genius-who-makes-the-world-cup-worth-watching/564443/.

Gonzalez, Roger. "Neymar Officially Joins PSG in World-Record Transfer Deal." CBS Sports, August 03, 2017. https://www.cbssports.com/soccer/news/neymar-officially-joins-psg-in-world-record-transfer-deal/.

"How Brilliant Is Paris's Neymar?" UEFA.com. Accessed on March 19, 2019. https://www.uefa.com/uefachampionsleague/news/newsid=2528644.html.

"How to Play Like Neymar in 15/16: 6 Ways to Do It." The18.com. Accessed on March 19, 2019. https://the18.com/news/how-to-play-like-Neymar-position-shoot-pass-dribble-defend.

"IOC Women and Sport Award Winners: Where Are They Now?" International Olympic Committee, March 18, 2019. https://www.olympic.org.

Jenkins, Michael. "Olympic Football 2012: Neymar Proving He's World's Best Young Footballer." Bleacher Report, August 12, 2017. https://bleacherreport.com/articles/1281914-neymar-using-the-olympics-to-show-he-is-the-best-young-player-in-the-world.

Jökulsson, Illugi. *Neymar: The New Pélé*. New York, NY: Abbeville Press Publishers, 2015.

"Juventus: UEFA Champions League Final." FC Barcelona. Accessed on March 18, 2019. www.fcbarcelona.com/en/matches/10444/juventus-fc-barcelona-uefa-champions-league-2014-15.

Keh, Andrew. "Neymar and the Art of the Dive." *New York Times*, July 5, 2018. https://www.nytimes.com/2018/07/05/sports/world-cup/neymar-brazil-diving.html.

Killon, Ann. *Champions of Men's Soccer*. New York, NY: Philomel Books, 2018.

Marsden, Sam. "Neymar's Skill 'Seems More Like Ballet Than Dribbling' –Luis Enrique." ESPN.com, May 6, 2017. http://www.espn.com/soccer/barcelona/story/3120709/neymars-skill-seems-more-like-ballet-than-dribbling-luis-enrique.

"Messi, Suárez, and Neymar Are the Most Lethal Trident in Europe." FC Barcelona. Accessed on March 19, 2019. https://www.fcbarcelona.com/en/news/769914/messi-suarez-and-neymar-are-the-most-lethal-trident-in-europe.

"Neymar." International Olympic Committee, May 23, 2017. https://www.olympic.org/neymar.

"Neymar Biography, Neymar Achievements, Neymar Career Stats." Edubilla.com. Accessed on March 19, 2019. http://www.edubilla.com/sport/football/players/neymar/.

Oldfield, Matt, and Tom Oldfield. *Neymar: From the Playground to the Pitch*. London, UK: Dino Books, 2018.

"Olympic Highlights 18/03/2019." International Olympic Committee, March 19, 2019. https://www.olympic.org/the-ioc.

"PSG 2–0 Strasbourg." FC Tables. Accessed on March 19, 2019. https://www.fctables.com/players/neymar-291274/.

Richards, Alex. "The 15 Best Wingers in World Football." Bleacher Report, October 3, 2017. https://bleacherreport.com/articles/1720086-the-15-best-wingers-in-world-football#slide13.

Smith, Rory. "In Orchestrating Barcelona Rally, Neymar Proves Ready for the Baton." *New York Times,* March 9, 2017. https://www.nytimes.com/2017/03/09/sports/soccer/champions-league-neymar-fc-barcelona-psg.html.

"Soccer Lingo Glossary." Sports Lingo, June 6, 2018. https://www.sportslingo.com/soccer-lingo-glossary/.

Southerland, Benjamin. *Neymar: A Biography of the Brazilian Superstar*. Chicago, IL: CreateSpace, 2016.

Trusdell, Brian. *Neymar: Soccer Superstar.* New York, NY: SportsZone, 2018.

Vignesh, Anuj. "Stars of the U-17 World Cup over the Years." ESPN.com, June 28, 2017. http://www.espn.com/soccer/u-17-world-cup/0/blog/post/3149268/from-buffon-to-neymar-stars-of-the-under-17-world-cup-over-the-years.

"Why Neymar Is Different." Medium, August 9, 2017. https://medium.com/@the_economist/why-neymar-is-different-44496ba4b0fe.

"World Cup: Neymar Leads Brazil Over Mexico 2–0 in Round of 16." Azcentral.com, July 2, 2018. https://www.azcentral.com/story/sports/soccer/worldcup/2018/07/02/live-updates-mexico-brazil/747444002/.

Index

Page numbers in **boldface** are images.

About the Author

Ruth Bjorklund has a master's degree in library and information science. She has written numerous books for young people on a variety of subjects—science, wildlife, geography, history, and contemporary issues. She lives on Bainbridge Island, a ferry ride away from Seattle, Washington. The Seattle Sounders are her soccer team, and after a win, when the fireworks are set off in the stadium, happy fans swarm the streets along the waterfront.